Friends Along the Way

by Alice Collins
illustrated by John Mantha

SCHOOL PUBLISHERS

Printed in China

ISBN 10:   0-15-377433-9
ISBN 13:   978-0-15-377433-1

Ordering Options
ISBN 10:   0-15-377149-6 (Grade 5 Collection)
ISBN 13:   978-0-15-377149-1 (Grade 5 Collection)
ISBN 10:   0-15-377892-X (package of 5)
ISBN 13:   978-0-15-377892-6 (package of 5)

2 3 4 5 6 7 8 9 10   0940   17 16 15 14 13 12 11 10 09

A Presidential Request

In 1803, President Thomas Jefferson asked Meriwether Lewis and William Clark to lead an expedition westward. This group, called the Corps of Discovery, would lead the first expedition to the Pacific Ocean. At

A Jefferson peace medal

that time, little was known about the land that lay between the Mississippi River and the Pacific Ocean. Jefferson asked Lewis and Clark's team to study the land intently.

It was well-known that several groups of Native Americans occupied the land west of the Mississippi River, and Jefferson knew that Lewis and Clark would encounter them along the way. He also knew that it would be a dangerous journey and wanted to keep the men out of peril. Jefferson wanted the Native Americans to know that Lewis and Clark's mission was peaceful. To ensure this, he gave peace medals to Lewis and Clark to present to each Native American chief they encountered along the way.

On their journey, the Corps of Discovery did meet various Native American tribes. Each of these groups helped the expedition in its own way. Without their help, Lewis and Clark's mission would not have been successful.

The Mandan and the Hidatsa

The first Native Americans to help the Corps of Discovery were the Mandan and the Hidatsa. Both of these groups lived in villages of earthen lodges in the Upper Missouri River Valley. This area is now North Dakota. Each village had a plaza in its center and was surrounded by a protective log wall.

Although both groups grew corn, tobacco, squash, and beans, the Mandan people were especially noted for their excellent corn. Each year, their Native American neighbors as well as European traders would come to the Mandan villages to trade goods for corn.

Unlike the Mandan, the Hidatsa were warlike. They were often at war with the Shoshone and Blackfeet. The Hidatsa considered a young man's success in battle to be a sign that he would make a good leader. They also fought for money, for revenge and to defend themselves.

Lewis and Clark's group built a fort near the Mandan. They planned to stay in it during the dismal winter months. "Fort Mandan" was set apart from the Mandan villages, but was close enough for the explorers to set up trade. The Mandans traded their food for goods.

The Mandan wanted to keep the Hidatsa and the explorers apart. They did not want the Hidatsa trading with the Americans and tried to turn the Hidatsa against the explorers. The Mandan told the Hidatsa that Lewis and Clark planned to raid their villages, which was not true.

In spite of their uneasy feelings toward the expedition, the Hidatsa did help the Americans, showing them a route to the Rocky Mountains. They also introduced them to Toussaint Charbonneau and his wife, Sacagawea.

Charbonneau, a French fur trader, knew the Hidatsa language and was hired by Lewis and Clark to be their interpreter. His wife, Sacagawea, was a Shoshone Native American who had been kidnapped years before by the Hidatsa. She had grown up with the Hidatsa and knew about crops and farming. Since she was a Shoshone, Lewis and Clark knew Sacagawea could be a real asset to the expedition.

In the spring of 1805, the expedition thanked both the Mandan and Hidatsa for their help and headed west. Charbonneau and Sacagawea and their young son were part of the group.

The Shoshone

The expedition met the Shoshone in August of 1805. At this time, Lewis and Clark and their group were still traveling on foot and hoping to find a waterway that would lead them across the Northwest to the Pacific Ocean.

The Shoshone who lived east of the Rocky Mountains had been buffalo hunters whose enemies had run them off of the plains and into the rugged mountain terrain. Without buffalo, they were living on berries, roots, fish, and small game.

While traveling through a mountain pass, the expedition came upon several Shoshone women who were gathering food. Never having seen explorers before, the Shoshone were afraid of these strangers. First Lewis approached them kindly and with gifts.

Even though the Shoshone did not possess a lot, they shared all they had, namely food and shelter, with the explorers. The Shoshone chief, Cameahwait, welcomed them. They became guests of the Shoshone. The chief also explained how to take a safe route through the mountains to the Columbia River. The explorers knew that for this leg of the journey, they would need horses.

Lewis and Clark met with the chief to talk about horses. At this time, Sacagawea was called in to translate. As a Shoshone, she understood the people. The explorers wanted her to get the best bargain for them. When Sacagawea entered and saw the chief, she couldn't believe her eyes. He was her brother! She had not seen him since she had been kidnapped by the Hidatsa when she was twelve years old. After a tearful reunion, her brother, Chief Cameahwait, agreed to sell the explorers the horses they needed to continue on their journey.

The Nez Perce

Thanks to Sacagawea and her Shoshone brother, the explorers crossed the Rocky Mountains on horseback. They moved into the territory that is now Montana and Idaho. There they met the Nez Perce, another group of Native Americans.

The Nez Perce lived on the west side of the Rocky Mountains. They owned one of the largest horse herds in North America. They were known as great horsemen. Like the Shoshone, the Nez Perce hunted buffalo.

Chief Twisted Hair welcomed Lewis and Clark and the Corps of Discovery and invited them to stay for several days. He explained the route ahead, and his tribe helped the explorers to make canoes. As they waited for the snows to melt, the two groups became friendly. The Nez Perce provided the Corps with food. In exchange for the food, Meriwether Lewis treated illnesses of the Nez Perce. He became their "favorite doctor."

The Chinook and the Clatsop

The Chinook and the
Clatsop were neighboring
Native American tribes that lived
along the Columbia River. The
Corps of Discovery met with both
groups in late 1805. By this
time, the expedition was
following the Columbia
River to the Pacific
Ocean. The Nez Perce
had warned the expedition
about the Chinook. They had
a different language and
culture than the other
Native American tribes.

Since the Chinook lived
along the river, they were excellent
canoe-builders and fishers. They
also had grown accustomed to trading
with the Europeans and Canadians in North America.
When they first met the Corps, the Chinook were
peaceful. In return, Lewis and Clark presented them
with medals, flags, and other trinkets.

Unfortunately, as time went on, the relationship
changed. The Chinook began to sell their food to the
Corps at high prices. The explorers began to lose
their trust in the Chinook.

On the other hand, the Corps held Chief Coboway and the Clatsop in high esteem, as they had helped the Corps survive the cold winter. The Clatsop had advised them on the best place to build their fort. When they left Fort Clatsop

to continue west, they left all their furniture behind as a gift for Chief Coboway and the Clatsop. In his journal, Lewis said that Chief Coboway had been the most kind and hospitable of all those he met in that region. He was particularly grateful to the Clatsop for providing them with the knowledge of where to find the best elk hunting.

The Walla Walla

The Walla Walla lived where the Snake and Columbia Rivers intersect in what is now southern Washington. Lewis and Clark first met them in October of 1805. Their first meeting was very brief, as the expedition was in a hurry to finally reach the Pacific Ocean. They did, however, promise the Walla Walla chief that they would return to his village on the way back.

The Walla Walla Chief Yelleppit gave Clark a white horse and the information he and the Corps needed to reach their final destination. He also gave them firewood, more horses, and canoes. In return, Clark gave Yelleppit his sword, ammunition, and other items that were of value to the tribe.

The visit with the Walla Walla ended with a huge party. The Walla Walla invited another tribe called the Yakima to join in the celebration. There was food, music, and dancing. Before leaving, the Americans thanked the Native American tribes profusely.

Friends Along the Way

The Lewis and Clark expedition had been an ordeal during which the Corps survived brutal weather, rough terrain, and endless setbacks. Even though Lewis and Clark decided to return home by a different route, they came across many of the same people they had met going west. In their journals, Lewis, Clark, and the other members of the expedition described in detail their experiences.

Lewis and Clark's journey was more than a remarkable adventure. Their expedition helped define the boundaries of our country. They created some of the first maps of the western United States based on their journey. They identified plants and animals that they found. They also reported on the Native Americans they met along the way. It is because of Lewis and Clark's journey that people from the East began to settle in the West. Their history-making journey might not have been possible had it not been for all of the "friends along the way."

Sacagawea and her son, Pompey, on the one dollar coin.

Think Critically

1. Why was it important that Lewis and Clark befriend the Native Americans along the way?

2. What words would you use to describe Lewis and Clark and the explorers of the Corps of Discovery?

3. Name at least three ways the Native Americans helped the expedition.

4. Summarize the main idea of this book.

5. Which Native American tribe would you have liked to have visited? Why?

 **Social Studies**

Draw a Map Look at a map of the United States. Using the information in the book and the map, draw your own map of the route Lewis and Clark took from Missouri to the Pacific Ocean. Remember which Native American tribes they met along the way and add them to your map.

School-Home Connection Tell your family about Lewis and Clark's expedition to the West. Then talk about expeditions you and your family have taken or would like to take.

Word Count: 1,570